P9-DBT-143

JEFF BEZOS

JEFF BEZOS

AMAZON.COM ARCHITECT

by Tom Robinson

Content Consultant:
Mohan Menon, PhD
Department of Marketing, University of South Alabama

ABDO
Publishing Company

CREDITS

Published by ABDO Publishing Company, 8000 West 78th Street, Edina, Minnesota 55439. Copyright © 2010 by Abdo Consulting Group, Inc. International copyrights reserved in all countries. No part of this book may be reproduced in any form without written permission from the publisher. The Essential Library™ is a trademark and logo of ABDO Publishing Company.

Printed in the United States.

 PRINTED ON RECYCLED PAPER

Editor: Rebecca Rowell
Copy Editor: Paula Lewis
Interior Design and Production: Becky Daum
Cover Design: Emily Love

Library of Congress Cataloging-in-Publication Data
Robinson, Tom, 1964–
  Jeff Bezos : Amazon.com architect / by Tom Robinson.
     p. cm. — (Publishing pioneers)
  Includes bibliographical references and index.
  ISBN 978-1-60453-759-8
  1. Bezos, Jeffrey—Juvenile literature. 2. Booksellers and bookselling—United States—Biography—Juvenile literature. 3. Businessmen—United States—Biography—Juvenile literature. 4. Amazon.com (Firm)—History—Juvenile literature. 5. Internet bookstores—United States—History—Juvenile literature. 6. Electronic commerce—United States—History—Juvenile literature. I. Title.
  Z473.B47R63 2010
  381'.4500202854678—dc22
  [B]

                                        2009015989

TABLE OF CONTENTS

In 1994, Jeff and MacKenzie Bezos left the life they knew in New York City to pursue Jeff's dream in Seattle, Washington.

Mapping Out a Plan

It was the summer of 1994. Millions of people throughout the United States were soaking in swimming pools, boating on lakes, grooming their yards, and enjoying other outdoor activities. Jeff and MacKenzie Bezos (pronounced

BAY-zoes) were focused on other matters. The young couple was making a big life change.

Jeff worked on Wall Street as a financial analyst for D. E. Shaw & Company, an investment firm. He had a technical degree from Princeton University and used his computer skills to help the company with stock trades.

By combining his understanding of computer science with financial investing, Bezos had landed a million-dollar-a-year job as an executive. His work with computers made Bezos quite aware of the Internet, which in the early 1990s was just beginning to become part of everyday life.

Inspiration

The Internet originated from the U.S. Defense Department's attempt to keep its computers communicating in the event of a nuclear attack. The system slowly evolved into a network over which college and government researchers could exchange information and messages across many computers.

Historians place the timeframe in which the Internet became a part of

"If you're not stubborn, you'll give up on experiments too soon. And if you're not flexible, you'll pound your head against the wall and you won't see a different solution to a problem you're trying to solve."[1]

—*Jeff Bezos*

society between September 1993 and March 1994. Bezos had first used the Internet while at Princeton University almost a decade earlier. By 1994, Internet usage, while growing, was still not much of a part of everyday life. To that point, it was hardly seen as a way to do business.

Bezos knew that to make people want to shop on the Internet, he had to come up with something special. "Unless you could create something with a huge value proposition for the customer, it would be easier for them to do it the old way," he said. He needed "to do something that simply cannot be done any other way."[2]

Dot-com Boom and Bust

The emergence of the Internet led to huge growth in companies designed to take advantage of the new technology. From the mid-1990s until approximately 2001, vast amounts of money were invested through the stock market in companies that hoped to make money from consumers' use of the Internet. The companies, many of which were created during this time, were referred to as "dot-coms." With investment money plentiful, these companies often spent freely in anticipation of eventual success.

Stock prices went up, largely because of the speculated value of these new companies. In turn, more people invested in the companies. Ultimately, many dot-coms, while innovative, were unable to generate profits through the Internet. They simply did not experience the success that had been hoped or projected. The lack of financial returns made investors uneasy. Many sold their stock, which made stock prices drop. In addition, new investment stopped. As a result, the value of many dot-coms crashed and, without new investment to keep trying new ideas, many of the companies went out of business.

In his research, Bezos learned that Internet use was increasing by more than 2,300 percent a year. He realized the day would come when that increased use would include a way to conduct business. He explained his realization:

> *The wake-up call was finding this startling statistic that web usage in the spring of 1994 was growing at 2,300 percent a year. You know, things just don't grow that fast. It's highly unusual, and that started me . . . thinking, "What kind of business plan might make sense in the context of that growth?"[3]*

At the time, the Internet had just started changing from a way to transfer messages and files—primarily through e-mail—to the World Wide Web, where information was posted and accessed. Early Web browsers allowed Internet users to easily type in a Web address or click a link to view a page for the first time. Businesses and public entities were responding by creating simple Web pages with information about their organizations. These pages contained virtually none of the interactive devices used today that make pages interesting to readers.

Bezos studied the top 20 mail-order businesses to determine if one seemed best suited for the

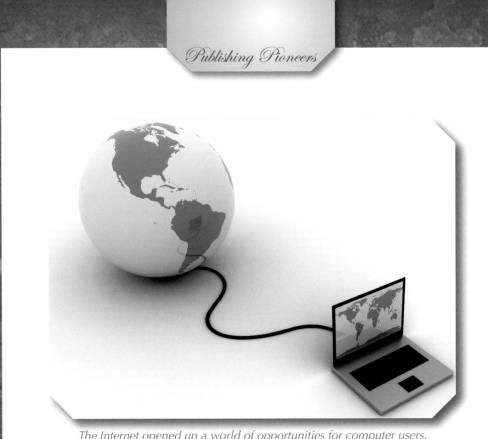

The Internet opened up a world of opportunities for computer users, including the possibility of shopping online.

Internet. As he considered the possibilities, Bezos began exploring the idea for books, which did not have a significant mail-order business in place. Marketing and selling books by mail order had not been successful. Creating a catalog of all available books was impractical due to the vast number of books available and the problem of how to categorize the products. The virtually limitless space on the Internet, however, suited such a listing of books. Two Internet booksellers did exist at the time—

CLBooks.com and Books.com—but Bezos still liked the idea of creating his own online bookstore.

Bezos needed to find out more about the book publishing industry. He flew to Los Angeles, California, to attend the convention of the American Booksellers' Association. His goal was to learn as much as possible. Bezos discovered his idea seemed practical. Booksellers had lists of inventory already in their computers. He would need a way to gather those lists.

A Final Decision

The plan Bezos was developing did not fit with D. E. Shaw & Company. The 30-year-old approached his boss, David Shaw, about his idea. It was a topic the two men had discussed previously. Shaw suggested that he and Bezos go for a walk. They spent two hours in Central Park. At the end of their conversation, Shaw told Bezos, "You know, this actually sounds like a really good idea to me, but it sounds like it would be a better idea for somebody who didn't already

Skeptical Names

During its early years, skeptics doubted that Amazon.com would be successful. The company was mocked in print in 1996 as Amazon.con, suggesting the company's financial plans could never work in the real world. The company was later referred to as both Amazon.toast and Amazon.bomb, suggesting the company was about to fail. Other skeptics called the company Amazon.org, implying it would not make a profit (the designation .org is used by nonprofit agencies).

have a good job."[4] Shaw suggested that Bezos take two days to make his final decision.

Jeff Bezos knew what he had to do. He and MacKenzie left New York City that summer of 1994 for a new home on the opposite coast. After flying to Houston, Texas, the home of Jeff's parents, the couple headed to Seattle, Washington. As MacKenzie drove the SUV her in-laws provided as a gift, Jeff typed eagerly on his laptop.

Bezos busily transferred his thoughts and ideas into his computer. It was the first draft of a master plan for a company that would become one of the biggest success stories of the dot-com era. Bezos was ready to create an online bookstore. He would not only help customers find books but also connect them with books they might not have been aware of otherwise. Upon his arrival in Seattle, Bezos went to work bringing his idea to life. Soon, retailing and publishing would change.

"So, you want to start a company. Well, the first thing you do is . . . write a business plan, . . . I wrote about a 30-page business plan. I wrote a first draft. . . . And, that is very helpful. You know the business plan won't survive its first encounters with reality. It will always be different. The reality will never be the plan, but the discipline of writing the plan forces you to think through some of the issues and to get sort of mentally comfortable in the space. Then you start to understand, if you push on this knob this will move over here and so on. So, that's the first step."[5]

—*Jeff Bezos*

Jeff Bezos holds Amazon.com's first sign.

Jeff Bezos was born in Albuquerque, New Mexico.

YOUNG JEFF

Jeffrey Preston Jorgensen was born on January 12, 1964, in Albuquerque, New Mexico, to Jacklyn Gise Jorgensen and Ted Jorgensen. Jackie was a young mother. Ted split with Jackie when Jeff was only one year old, and the couple later divorced. Jeff has no memory of his biological father.

Jeff's determination and resourcefulness were apparent when he was quite young. When he was three years old, Jeff no longer wanted to sleep in a crib. He wanted his own bed, but his mother resisted. One day, Jackie found her little boy playing with a screwdriver. Jeff was working on the crib, trying to take it apart himself to turn it into a bed.

Others also noticed Jeff's persistence. Teachers at his Montessori preschool noted that once Jeff was involved in a project, his concentration became so intense that they would have to lift him up, chair and all, to move on to the next activity.

When Jeff was four years old, his mother married Miguel "Mike" Bezos. He adopted Jeff, whose last name then became Bezos. Mike Bezos shared his love of science with the brilliant and inquisitive youngster. Soon, Jeff had siblings. Within two years, the Bezos family grew with the births of Christina and Mark, Jeff's younger sister and brother.

Jackie Gise Bezos

Jackie Gise was a teenager when she gave birth to her first son, Jeff, and divorced Ted Jorgensen. Jeff was born two weeks after Jackie's seventeenth birthday, when she was still in high school. Jackie went on to graduate from high school and a community college. She then took a job as a bookkeeper at the Bank of New Mexico. While working at the bank, Jackie met Mike Bezos, whom she married in 1968.

SUMMERS ON THE RANCH

Before retiring, Lawrence Preston Gise, Jeff's grandfather, worked as regional director of the Atomic Energy Commission, where he had been responsible for a staff of 26,000. He moved to the Lazy G ranch in Cotulla, Texas, 90 miles (145 km) southwest of San Antonio. From the age of four through his mid-teen years, Jeff spent summers with his grandfather in Texas on the ranch.

An intelligent, hardworking man, Gise was able to show his grandson the high-tech world and life on a ranch at the same time. Together, Jeff and his grandfather built an automatic gate opener. They also fixed the D6 Caterpillar tractor when it needed repairs. Gise taught Jeff other skills, including how to weld metals and how to brand cattle.

Life on a ranch can be an adventurous time for a young child. Jeff's mother believed it was part of her son's vast education. "One of

On the Field

During his youth in Texas, Jeff Bezos did not have the ideal physical stature for football, a sport many Texans love. He barely met the minimum weight requirement. His mother, however, thought it was important that Jeff try activities other than the science projects with which he was so comfortable.

Undersized and inexperienced in the sport relative to the other players in the youth league, Jeff still found some success. He memorized all of the team's plays—both offensive and defensive—and he was made captain of the defense because he could also remember the responsibilities of all his teammates and help keep them positioned properly.

As a child, Jeff began spending summers on a ranch in Texas.

the things he learned is that there really aren't any problems without solutions," Jackie Bezos said. "Obstacles are only obstacles if you think they're obstacles. Otherwise, they're opportunities."[1]

A New Home

Although he returned to the ranch each summer, Jeff and his family were on the move throughout his childhood. Mike Bezos moved his wife and children from Albuquerque to Houston, Texas, where he took a job as an engineer for Exxon.

In school, Jeff was given a standardized test that confirmed his high intelligence. He was enrolled in River Oaks Elementary School because of its pilot program for gifted students. Attending the school required Jeff to take a daily 40-mile (64-km) ride roundtrip for three years of elementary school.

Coming from Cuba

Miguel "Mike" Bezos was 15 years old when he fled Cuba in 1962. He was one of more than 14,000 youngsters rescued by Operation Pedro Pan just before the Cuban Missile Crisis. At the time, many Cuban families found it preferable to get their children away from their homeland. Children were sent to church-run group homes and orphanages with the hope they would ultimately find a better life than if they remained in Cuba under the influence of Fidel Castro's Communist government.

Mike Bezos arrived in the United States with two shirts, including the one he was wearing, and one pair of pants. He did not speak English. He moved from Florida to a Catholic mission in Delaware, where he lived with 15 other Cuban refugees. Mike completed high school in Delaware and made his way to New Mexico and the University of Albuquerque, which offered scholarships to Cuban refugees. While attending college, the young Cuban worked the night shift at the Bank of New Mexico. That is where he met Jeff's mother.

Jeff was also challenged at home. His parents bought him science kits, which he worked on as a hobby. These entertained and taught him. There were times when Jeff did not need to follow the instructions provided in a science kit in order to work on projects. At River Oaks, he became enthralled with the

Infinity Cube, a cube with motorized mirrors that made it capable of sending multiple reflections in many directions. When Jackie Bezos determined that $20 was too much for such a toy, Jeff had a solution. The resourceful boy obtained parts much more cheaply and built his own version of the cube.

Glasses

When Jeff Bezos was ten years old, he learned he would have to wear glasses. In an interview as an adult, Bezos said that news was much more upsetting than learning that Mike Bezos was not his biological father.

Jeff's aptitude for science and building became apparent in other ways. River Oaks had a Teletype machine that could be connected to a mainframe computer by a modem. The teachers did not know how to use the machine, but Jeff and a few other students figured it out and programmed it for use.

Jeff found other uses for his abilities. With a little brother and sister in the house, he managed to protect his privacy by creating an alarm system on his bedroom door. A buzzer warned him when others, including his siblings, entered his room.

Dad

Mike and Jackie Bezos sat Jeff down when he was ten years old to explain that Mike was not Jeff's biological father. The news did not make a

Spring Cleaning

While growing up, Jeff Bezos moved frequently as his father was transferred to new positions while working for Exxon. Although moving usually means starting over in a new city and making new friends, Jeff was not daunted by these challenges. Rather, he thought of moving positively. "Moves always invigorated me," Bezos said, looking back at his childhood. "There's really something very cleansing about it. Every move is an opportunity for spring cleaning."[3]

difference in Jeff's life. Mike was the only father Jeff had ever known, and he respected Mike as a hardworking man who cared for his family.

The issue of who his blood relations are has seldom been a factor. "I've never met him," Jeff Bezos said of Ted Jorgensen. "But the reality, as far as I'm concerned, is that my Dad [Mike] is my natural father. The only time I ever think about it, genuinely, is when a doctor asks me to fill out a form."[2]

As Mike Bezos moved up through the ranks at Exxon, the family needed to relocate. When the Bezos family moved to Miami, Florida, Jeff often could be found in the garage working on various science projects. His tinkering foreshadowed the day when Jeff would build his own company from the ground up, largely from the garage of his Seattle home.

Jeff spent a lot of time as a teenager tinkering in the family's garage.

Jeff's love of technology and space made him a fan of the television series Star Trek.

EDUCATION

As a child, Jeff Bezos showed high intelligence and a distinct aptitude for science. Not surprisingly, he was enthralled by space as a teenager. *Star Trek* was his favorite television show. When he thought about his future, Jeff pictured himself as an astronaut or a physicist. His favorite book at the time was *Stranger in a Strange Land,* a novel about a human raised by martians on Mars.

The tinkering Jeff enjoyed as a child continued into his teens. Jeff transformed the Bezos family garage into a laboratory that often had a space theme. His many projects included trying to turn a vacuum cleaner into a hovercraft.

The curiosity and intelligence Jeff exhibited through his inventions continued to carry over into his schoolwork. He attended Palmetto Senior High and excelled as a student. While still in high school, he attended the Student Science Training Program at the University of Florida.

Although Jeff was quite talented, he did not always fit in as a high school student. But he became more comfortable socially when he spent time with other intellectually gifted people. That was the case with his first serious girlfriend. Ursula "Uschi" Werner was a grade ahead of Jeff. The two brilliant minds were strong competition for each other in the word game Boggle. She graduated first in her high school class and moved on to Duke University on

"I've always been at the intersection of computers and whatever they can revolutionize."[1]

—*Jeff Bezos*

High School Honors

When Jeff gave his high school valedictory speech at graduation in 1982, he used the opportunity to share his dream of one day colonizing outer space. The dream included building hotels and amusement parks in space.

a full scholarship on her way to becoming a Rhodes Scholar.

Jeff received several honors while in high school. He was named Best Science Student in his sophomore, junior, and senior years and Best Math Student as a junior and a senior. Jeff received a Silver Knight Award for excelling in academics and community service. He also served as class president. Jeff's final high school honor was being named valedictorian of his graduating class of 680 students.

Teaching Others

Following graduation from high school, Jeff found a summer job—by creating one. Jeff and Uschi partnered to develop a summer education "camp" out of his room. They called the camp the DREAM Institute. The name DREAM came from a combination of the first parts of the words *directed reasoning method*.

Jeff and Uschi sold the parents of five students in grades four, five, and six on the idea of paying $150 each for their children to attend two weeks of three-hour morning sessions. The institute included science studies and readings from books. "We don't just teach them something," Jeff said in an interview with the *Miami Herald*. "We ask them to apply it."[2]

PRINCETON UNIVERSITY

Following the summer of his DREAM Institute, Jeff headed off to Princeton University. He selected Princeton with the intention of studying theoretical physics, a subject that applies mathematics to nature in an attempt to better understand the world.

At Princeton, Jeff experienced something new.

Princeton University

Princeton University is in Princeton, New Jersey, which is located approximately halfway between New York City and Philadelphia, Pennsylvania. It is the fourth-oldest college in the United States. The school began as the College of New Jersey in Elizabeth in 1746. A year later, it moved to Newark. In 1756, the college moved again, to Princeton. There, the entire school was located in Nassau Hall for almost 50 years. Nassau Hall was the temporary capitol of the United States for a time in 1783. The school was officially named Princeton University in 1896, and a graduate school was added four years later. In 2009, the school enrolled approximately 5,000 undergraduate and 2,300 graduate students.

The Ivy League school has an impeccable reputation in physics, the field of study Jeff Bezos initially pursued. Albert Einstein, one of history's most famous scientists, moved to the United States when he left Nazi Germany in 1933 to take a position as professor of theoretical physics at Princeton. Nine members of Princeton's faculty and staff and eight alumni have been awarded the Nobel Prize for physics.

For the first time, he was matched up with students who, at least in the area of theoretical physics, were superior to him. Jeff said of the experience:

I looked around the room and it was clear to me that there were three people in the class who were much, much better at it than I was, and it was much, much easier for them. It was really sort of a startling insight, that there were people whose brains were wired differently.[3]

Although he had planned on studying theoretical physics, Jeff changed his major to computer science and electrical engineering.

The change in majors marked the beginning of using his analytical mind and understanding of computers to prepare himself to thrive professionally. In college, Jeff once again excelled as a student. In the spring of 1986 he graduated summa cum laude, which is Latin for "with highest praise."

A Phi Beta Kappan

Jeff Bezos was a Phi Beta Kappa graduate of Princeton University. Each year, approximately 1 in 100 college students in the arts and sciences is invited to join Phi Beta Kappa, the oldest academic honor society in the United States. Approximately 10 percent of the nation's colleges have Phi Beta Kappa chapters, and approximately 10 percent of the arts and sciences graduates of those schools are chosen for membership. According to Phi Beta Kappa, the ideal candidate "has demonstrated intellectual integrity, tolerance for other views, and a broad range of academic interests."[4]

Jeff's intelligence, curiosity, and determination were a good fit
with Princeton University.

In 1986, Jeff Bezos was faced with decisions regarding work. Because he was graduating from college, he would have to find a job.

FINDING WORK AND LOVE

As a senior at Princeton nearing graduation, Jeff Bezos was busy finishing his course work and actively looking for employment. He interviewed with well-established, successful companies such as Intel, Bell Labs, and

Andersen Consulting. Each of the companies offered Bezos a job, but he declined them.

Princeton's newspaper, the *Daily Princetonian*, had published a full-page advertisement for a company seeking the school's top graduates in computer science. Fitel was a start-up company building a worldwide telecommunications network that would make international business trading easier.

Bezos applied for a job with Fitel. He was an ideal candidate and was offered employment. This time, Bezos decided to accept the job offer. He was the eleventh employee hired by the company, which he joined after graduation. He started his professional career working in areas that combined computer science and business. Bezos used computer science to study market trends on Wall Street.

LIFE IN THE FAST LANE

The 23-year-old Bezos was managing accounts for clients worldwide—in England, Japan, and Australia. Much of his work was done using high-speed computer networking, but he was not at his desk all day. He flew around the world to set up accounts. He traveled to London, England, almost weekly.

The Laugh

A creative description of the Jeff Bezos laugh has become practically a required part of every newspaper and magazine profile written about the entrepreneur. Among the most repeated of those descriptions is one from *Time* magazine, which named Bezos its Person of the Year in 1999. *Time* described the laugh as "a rapid honk that sounds like a flock of Canadian geese on nitrous oxide."[2]

Bezos worked with Fitel a short time. Within two years, he was off to his next challenge. In April 1988, Bezos joined Bankers Trust Company. Less than one year later, he became the youngest vice president in company history. Bezos managed the programming department, which was responsible for designing a communications network.

Bezos was successful in what he called first-phase automation, the process of making technology work faster and more efficiently. As he prospered, the young man looked forward to greater challenges. His goal was to move to second-phase automation, which he described as where "you fundamentally change the underlying business process and do things in a completely new way. So it's more of a revolution instead of an evolution."[1]

ONE MORE STOP

In 1990, Bezos changed jobs again. Late that year, he accepted a position as vice president at D. E. Shaw & Company, a firm that handled investments.

The company specialized in applying computer science to the stock market.

In less than two years' time, he was elevated to the position of senior vice president. The title carried with it earnings of approximately $1 million, including stock options. As senior vice president, Bezos managed a 24-person department that explored and secured new markets.

MAKING A CONNECTION

One of Bezos's most distinct personal characteristics is a loud, honking laugh. It is impossible not to notice, which MacKenzie Tuttle discovered when

MacKenzie Bezos

MacKenzie Bezos was an aspiring writer and a recent Princeton University graduate when she went to work at D. E. Shaw & Company. While at Princeton, MacKenzie studied creative writing with Nobel Laureate Toni Morrison. In 2005, MacKenzie released a novel. She said of writing *The Testing of Luther Albright*, "I basically started this one in earnest in 1997. . . . I rewrote it so many times . . . and tried out a lot of differing points of view. So in some respects, I guess I wrote three or four novels—but none that I would've tried to publish."[3]

HarperCollins published *The Testing of Luther Albright* in 2005. The publisher provided the following information about the book: "Luther Albright is a devoted father and a designer of dams, a self-controlled man who believes he can engineer happiness for his family by sheltering them from his own emotions. But when an earthquake shakes his Sacramento home, the world Luther has constructed with such care begins to tilt. . . . This is a harrowing portrait of an ordinary man who finds himself tested and strives not to be found wanting."[4]

she worked at D. E. Shaw & Company. Her office was next to Bezos's—it was impossible not to hear him.

At the time MacKenzie joined the company as a researcher, Bezos was dating often. He encouraged friends to set him up on blind dates with the hope that he would find the woman who would be the right person for him. Instead, Bezos found her working for him.

A connection developed between Bezos and Tuttle in 1992, but that created a dilemma for Bezos. Because he was the supervisor of the unit in which MacKenzie worked, a romantic gesture from him could be misinterpreted—others might think he was taking advantage of his power.

But the mutual interest that developed after Tuttle began working at D. E. Shaw & Company grew to the point where she approached him. The couple began dating and, in 1993, they married.

Together, Jeff and MacKenzie would follow Jeff's dreams. He had an idea that would affect countless lives and change retailing and publishing.

Big Laughers

Jeff and MacKenzie now have four children: a daughter adopted from China and three sons. The laughter that first attracted MacKenzie to Jeff continues with the couple's children. "All of our kids are big laughers, as you would expect with a goofy dad like that," MacKenzie said. "There is a lot of laughter in our household."[5]

*Jeff Bezos had a successful career on Wall Street
before starting his own business.*

Jeff Bezos saw the possibilities of the Internet for retail.

FOLLOWING A DREAM

As a senior vice president at D. E. Shaw & Company, Jeff Bezos had a variety of duties. One responsibility was to study the Internet. The Internet was growing, and Bezos needed to keep current with the new technology. Bezos's examination of the Internet made him realize its potential for commerce. Closer studying helped him determine the selling of books as the way to make that first significant venture into Internet sales.

The Internet was enjoying a remarkable growth spurt when Bezos was assigned to monitor its progress. Hyperlinks allowed pointing and clicking to move quickly from one Web page to another. This was followed by the creation of Mosaic by University of Illinois students in 1993. It was the first Web browser to be widely used—on both PCs and Macs.

The Internet was opening up to easier access for a vastly increasing number of users. Bezos read one credible estimate that stated Internet use was growing at an annual rate of 2,300 percent because of Mosaic's availability on both Mac computers and Windows-based PCs. In his view, this created opportunities that he simply could not afford to miss.

"You have to keep in mind that human beings aren't good at

Working with Computers

Jeff Bezos spoke about being drawn to computer science: "I don't know. I think it's always hard to know why you're drawn to a particular thing. I think part of it is if you have a facility with that thing, of course it's satisfying to do it and so in a way that's self-reinforcing. And, certainly I always had a facility with computers. I always got along well with them and they're such extraordinary tools. You can teach them to do things and then they actually do them. It's kind of an incredible tool that we've built here in the 20th Century."[1]

understanding exponential growth," Bezos said.
"It's just not something we see in our everyday life."[2]
He described that type of growth as something that
doesn't happen "outside of petri dishes," but when
it does occur, something is "invisible today and
ubiquitous tomorrow."[3]

DECISION TIME

Bezos had a decision to make. He needed to
choose between staying at D. E. Shaw & Company
and pursuing his business idea. His position as
senior vice president was certain and provided Bezos
with a high income. If he gave up his job working for
David Shaw, Bezos would be taking a huge financial
risk. Pursuing his idea would require time and money. If it proved unsuccessful, Bezos would be without a job and likely without money in savings.

David Shaw urged Bezos to think one more time about whether he was ready to leave his job in New York City to launch his own company. Bezos analyzed what the decision would mean to his life as a whole:

Avid Reader

As a child, Jeff Bezos was an avid reader. Bezos explained, "I was very difficult to punish for my parents because they would send me to my room, and I was always happy to go to my room because I would just read. 'You're grounded and you have to stay in your room.' That was always fine with me. I was a big reader."[4]

I knew that when I was 80 I was not going to regret having
tried this. I was not going to regret trying to participate in this
thing called the Internet that I thought was going to be a really
big deal. I knew that if I failed I wouldn't regret that, but I
knew the one thing I might regret is not ever having tried. I
knew that that would haunt me every day, and so, when I
thought about it that way it was an incredibly easy decision.[5]

STARTING FROM SCRATCH

Bezos knew what he had to do. He quit his
lucrative job on Wall Street. He and MacKenzie
made the decision to leave New York City and head
to the opposite coast. They risked financial security
when Jeff gave up a budding career in a secure
industry. His family's financial future would be
at stake as he tried to prove his idea could make a
difference in the way people bought books. Jeff gave
up his steady and impressive income for the chance
to build something bigger, all while draining what
money he had built up.

Jeff and MacKenzie moved to Seattle,
Washington, where Jeff launched his business in his
garage. He selected Seattle as a launch location for
a few reasons. Bezos had a close friend there who

Jeff and MacKenzie Bezos headed to Seattle to start an online bookstore.

strongly recommended the city. In addition, Seattle was one of the early hot spots of the Internet industry and had more skilled computer workers than other areas. It was also close to the home of Ingram Book Group, a wholesale book company based across the border in Roseburg, Oregon.

New Home for a New Business

Jeff and MacKenzie Bezos rented a small house. They ran extension cords from the house into the garage. Using doors as the top surface, Jeff built tables and desks for less than $60 each and set up computers on them. In an era when programmers had to write even the most basic of codes to run each part of a computer application, Bezos went about the tedious process of building a Web site.

Although book companies had databases of book listings, combining those lists and adding the elements his company would use for its searches was a time-consuming task. Shel Kaphan, one of Bezos's first employees, described that process as being similar to emptying a swimming pool with a straw.

Bezos originally incorporated his new company as Cadabra, Inc. on July 5, 1994. The name was a shortened form of *abracadabra*, a word borrowed from magic. He later changed the name. His main reason for making the change was because a friend heard the word *cadaver*, not *Cadabra*, during a telephone conversation. Others might hear the same word, which likely would not be good for business. The company's new name, Amazon.com, had both practical and symbolic meaning for Bezos.

Yahoo!, the top Internet search engine at the time, was listing search results alphabetically, so it was helpful for a business to have a name beginning with the letter *A*. And in a comparison with how the Internet as a whole worked, Bezos named the company after the South American river with its many branches.

The first Amazon.com office and warehouse were in the garage of Jeff and MacKenzie's rented house in Bellevue, an eastern suburb of Seattle. Jeff purchased the original $10,000 in company stock and loaned the company $15,000 to officially start the operation with $25,000. It was the beginning of using family money—initially from Jeff and MacKenzie, then from Jeff's parents—to get Amazon.com through its early stages. Months later, in November 1994, Bezos took money from personal funds again, loaning the company another $29,000.

The first Amazon.com workforce was created with Shel Kaphan and Paul Barton-Davis. They joined Jeff in development while MacKenzie took on the multiple roles of accountant, secretary, and office manager. Amazon.com's inventory came from Ingram Book Group. Jeff Bezos and his small band of employees all packaged the books for shipping. They worked late into the night to fill the orders themselves before Bezos would rush them to UPS.

The new company name, Amazon.com, was registered on February 9, 1995. Bezos's parents were his major investors, putting up approximately

$300,000—the bulk of their savings and retirement money. Amazon.com was on its way.

Changing the Market

When Bezos was finally ready to test Amazon.com, he contacted hundreds of friends and business acquaintances to check it out. He saw what he wanted to see—his site would work on a variety of computers. On July 16, 1995, just over one year after moving to Seattle to pursue his dream, Bezos was ready to show his site to the rest of the world. To keep costs down, he went back to the same people who had tested the site and asked them to spread the word. Within a month, he

Packing Tables

In an interview with the Academy of Achievement, Jeff Bezos discussed his company's beginnings and the work involved in meeting customer demands:

We had so many orders that we weren't ready for, that we had no real organization in our distribution center at all. In fact, we were packing on our hands and knees on a hard concrete floor. I remember, just to show you how stupid I can be—my only defense is that it was late. We were packing these things, everybody in the company and I had this brainstorm as I said to the person next to me, "This packing is killing me! My back hurts, this is killing my knees on this hard cement floor" and this person said, "Yeah, I know what you mean." And I said, "You know what we need?" my brilliant insight, "We need knee pads!" I was very serious, and this person looked at me like I was the stupidest person they'd ever seen. I'm working for this person? This is great. "What we need is packing tables."[6]

UPS

When his company started, Jeff Bezos took orders that were ready to be shipped to his local UPS office. He explained, "I would drive these things to UPS so we could get the last one, and we would wait till the last second. I'd get to UPS and I would sort of bang on the glass door that was closed. They would always take pity on me and sort of open up and let us ship things late."[8]

was selling books in every U.S. state and around the world.

The way books are sold has changed as a result of Amazon.com. Established bookselling companies followed Amazon.com into the online world. "A very successful, profitable, midlist book might sell 15,000 copies," Bezos said. "In the old world, finding the right 15,000 people to buy that book was ridiculously expensive. This is something that Amazon.com and the Internet, in general, have really helped with."[7]

Jeff Bezos helped create online retailing with Amazon.com.

Research and foresight led Jeff Bezos to focus on becoming an online bookseller.

CREATING A
SUCCESSFUL PRODUCT

Jeff Bezos capitalized on the Internet to create a new retailing opportunity with Amazon.com. By September 1995, two months after its debut, Amazon.com was selling $20,000 worth of books each week. Bezos believed customer service was the key to success, and his focus was on that rather than profits. He wanted to get big fast. In fact, that became his motto.

Following its launch, Amazon.com continued to take advantage of computer technology to improve customer service. To maintain communication between the company and its customers, orders were verified through e-mail, and customer reviews were added to the site. The online bookstore also created features to improve the user experience. In September 1997, 1-Click shopping was added to make shopping even easier for returning customers. Such features were a hit with customers. Those customers then spread positive word about the company, and their friends began to check it out. From the start, Amazon.com advertised much less than similarly sized businesses. Bezos operated under the premise that if a company offered excellent service, people would find out.

Originally, Bezos had run into many advisors who suggested he not

1-Click Shopping

Amazon.com introduced its 1-Click shopping in September 1997 to improve its online shopping experience. The tool allows repeat shoppers the ability to complete their transactions with the click of a single button. Before the advent of 1-Click shopping, users had to complete an online order form each time they returned to an online retailer to make a purchase.

Slogans

Jeff Bezos uses sayings at work to encourage himself and his employees. One commonly heard from Bezos after launching Amazon.com was "sacrifice the present for a better future." Others include "work hard, have fun, make history" and "ideas are easy, it's execution that's hard."[1]

The slogans and inspirational messages from Bezos are never far from sight for Amazon.com workers. They are on posters on walls throughout the company's buildings. Whiteboards are found on many walls and inside elevators so messages can be shared among employees.

even try to sell books online. Those who acknowledged that the effort might be worthwhile cautioned that he should not try to sell more than 300,000 titles. Bezos wanted to make as many books as possible available and sought out 1 million titles to offer on the site. Through Amazon.com, readers found more options, which became another strength of the business.

With Amazon.com's help, users were being connected to titles they might never have learned about or considered. Books that once might have bordered on being impractical for publishers to produce and sell were more frequently making their ways into the hands of readers who once might not have taken the time to locate them. In an industry where profit per sale is low, less money was now needed to market a product. This made profit more likely for a publisher and reasonable costs more likely for a consumer.

The way Bezos viewed doing business was to gain as large a share of the market as possible and then treat those customers better than anyone else would treat them. He believed this would ensure his company's success in the long run. If he could find a way to attract more customers and turn them into happier customers, the money would follow.

And the money did follow—even in Amazon.com's inaugural year. The company's first year in business, which was only July through December,

Mosaic

Mosaic was a Web browser developed by students at the National Center for Supercomputer Applications (NCSA) at the University of Illinois. It was not the first Web browser ever created, but it was the first used widely. Mosaic's first version for PCs, 0.5, was released in January 1993. Mosaic for Macs came out later that year. By November 1993, version 1.0 of Mosaic took off with Internet users. What made the software popular was its use of icons, bookmarks, pictures, and other features that made the Web more manageable to people who were not necessarily technologically savvy.

Mosaic was available at no cost from the NCSA Web site. More than 5,000 copies were soon downloaded monthly. Growth was exponential, resulting in millions of global users by 1994. Within a few years, however, the browser landscape changed. The software quickly developed into new programs, including the once-popular Netscape Web browser. Dozens of companies licensed their own versions of browser software. In 1997, the NCSA moved on from the project, abandoning Mosaic for other research interests. Although the project ended after only a few years, the effects of Mosaic are felt daily. The browser created new communication opportunities for people worldwide. It also allowed online retail businesses such as Amazon.com to exist.

Following his company's initial success, Jeff Bezos was concerned about Amazon.com's ability to keep up with customers' orders.

was a success in that Amazon.com had $511,000 in sales in 1995. However, Amazon.com's expenses exceeded its sales, which is common for start-up companies. As a result, the company had a net loss of $303,000 that year. More money was needed to keep the company going. In 1995, Bezos successfully pitched his company to more than 20 venture capitalists. They liked the idea and contributed $981,000 to Amazon.com in December of that year.

GROWING PAINS

Even with its initial sales success and additional investors, Bezos had concerns. The young entrepreneur could now see his business succeeding in some key areas, but still not bringing in more money than the enormous costs of growing to meet customer demands. If Amazon.com could not meet the orders and serve the customers well, Bezos feared he would lose those customers.

Early plans for Amazon.com called for concentrating on customer service and ordering, with the shipping handled by others. However, the orders came in so quickly that Amazon.com responded directly to the orders. The early days of the dot-com business featured computer experts packing boxes into the late hours of the night to meet shipping demands until more staff could be hired. The garage was no longer large enough to handle the shipping part of the operation. The company moved to a new location to have enough space to get the work done.

The Bezos Routine

Jeff Bezos usually starts his day between 7:00 a.m. and 8:00 a.m. Before heading to the office, Bezos exercises on his treadmill. While exercising, he reads the morning newspapers. At work, Bezos tries to avoid being in his office all day. He attends meetings and checks on activities in the building. He usually works until 7:00 p.m. During each quarter of the year, Bezos takes a three-day break. He spends time alone at a hotel to think about what to do next at work.

Amazon.com's Books

Although he did not hesitate to sell the most popular books, what Bezos ultimately created was a way to connect books that did not necessarily make bestseller lists with readers who found them useful. "Relative to the industry as a whole, we're disproportionately weighed toward harder-to-find titles," Bezos said. "People sometimes confuse obscurity with bad quality."[3]

As much as he has always loved science, numbers, and computers, Bezos has also believed in following a gut feeling. He kept pushing the financial risks to the limit because he believed in the potential for a positive result. This brought Bezos—and the company—to the brink of bankruptcy. He was insolvent, without a net worth, because he owed more money than he possessed.

But Amazon.com had experienced a successful start, and that success was not the result of happenstance. The new company had taken the lead in the online world by making shopping convenient, providing quality customer service, and making previously unavailable information about books available to its customers. As competitors tried to catch up, Bezos implored his dedicated workforce to keep finding ways to make the company more effective. "Our mission is to invent and innovate on behalf of our customers," he said.[2] The challenge now was to stay ahead.

Jeff Bezos knew the Internet was a good medium for retail.

Amazon.com employees are busy filling orders.

BUSINESS SUCCESS

The way customers purchased and searched for books changed with the growth of Amazon.com, which earned recognition as the world's number one e-tailer, a term created to describe retailers on the Internet. *Forbes* covers such topics as personal finance and investing in the stock market. The magazine wrote, "Amazon is the first shining ray of the new commercial millennium. . . . It's the shape of business in the next century."[1]

COMPUTERS AND HUMANS

Bezos not only grasped the concept of interaction between humans and computers, but he also recognized the differences between the two. Programs on Amazon.com recommend books to consumers based on their past purchases. Suggestions made by humans would yield books with obvious connections. The Amazon.com programs found some surprising trends. Bezos explained:

> I remember one of the first times this struck me. The main book on the page was on Zen. There were other suggestions for Zen books, and in the middle of those was a book on how to have a clutter-free desk. That's not something that a human editor would have ever picked. But statistically, the people who were interested in Zen books also wanted clutter-free desks.[2]

Computers can perform the multitude of calculations needed to quickly process large amounts of information. The ability of a computer program to sort through vast data and spot a statistical trend is sometimes referred to as "artificial intelligence." Bezos also recognized areas where humans were more proficient than computers, something he liked to call artificial artificial intelligence (AAI). Sorting photos of items based on small differences is one such area of AAI. Bezos used the concept of AAI to have humans take over for the computer

Milestone

In October 1997, Amazon.com filled its one millionth order. Bezos personally delivered the two books that were part of that order to Japan.

in these areas and arranged this work in a program he called Amazon Mechanical Turk. Through the Amazon Mechanical Turk Web site (www.mturk. com), companies can post projects that need to be done, and workers can sign up for a chance to complete those human intelligence tasks (HITs).

INTERESTED INVESTORS

Bezos continued to study and appraise his company's situation, online retailing, and what customers seemed to want and need. His constant focus on improving his business and pleasing those who shopped at Amazon.com did not go unnoticed.

Ramanan Raghavendran was a senior associate with General Atlantic Partners, a private equity firm in Greenwich, Connecticut. Early in 1996, Raghavendran was surfing the World Wide Web when he happened upon Amazon.com. Raghavendran's job at General Atlantic was to pursue Internet-related investments for his company. He was so interested by what he saw that he telephoned Bezos.

Private equity firms often look at financially struggling companies that otherwise have value. By investing in such companies, the private equity firms gain control of some company stock, which they hope will become more valuable through using the new investment to reorganize the company. An increase in the value of company stock can result in a huge return on the equity firms' investment should they decide to sell the stock.

Raghavendran called Bezos, which encouraged the entrepreneur and the top managers at Amazon. com to be open to the prospects of public investing. If the company was

Person of the Year

Years before Amazon. com turned its first profit, *Time* magazine named Jeff Bezos its Person of the Year for 1999. Recognizing Bezos as the king of cyber commerce just five years after he headed to Seattle to launch Amazon.com, *Time* made him the fourth-youngest person ever selected for the prestigious award. The only people younger than Bezos had been Charles Lindbergh, Queen Elizabeth II, and Martin Luther King Jr.

impressive enough to draw unsolicited investment inquiries from General Atlantic, then the opportunity to raise larger amounts of money was probably available. This would allow the continued concentration on getting bigger first rather than emphasizing a profit margin.

A May 16, 1996, story in the *Wall Street Journal* helped Amazon.com garner the attention of more customers and more potential investors. A year later, on May 15, 1997, Bezos was ready to take his company public. The process of getting public investors through Wall Street to expand a successful company, and in turn do even more business, created a financial payoff that made Bezos and his parents billionaires. Going public raised $54 million for Amazon.com. Although Bezos was confident in his idea, he had warned early investors, including his parents, that there was approximately a 70 percent chance of failure and the loss of the entire investment. "We weren't betting on the Internet," Bezos's mother said. "We were betting on Jeff."[3]

The return on the original investment and the additional money brought in through the sale of company shares brought financial security back to Jeff and MacKenzie Bezos. But that still was not

*Jeff Bezos had to find investors with a lot of money
to help Amazon.com survive and thrive.*

proof that Amazon.com could make a consistent
profit. Cutting costs for customers and publishers
still needed to be translated into a profit margin for
the Internet retailer. As customer demands grew
rapidly, so did the costs of serving those customers.

After extensive negotiations, Amazon.com
selected the California firm Kleiner Perkins
Caulfield & Byers for venture capital rather than
General Atlantic. The firm invested $8 million
while agreeing to value Amazon.com at $60 million.
This gave Kleiner Perkins Caulfield & Byers
approximately 13 percent of the company stock.

For Jeff Bezos and his company to be successful, there was still work to be done. Bezos was trying to change the way customers did business. Such changes were not going to happen without drastic measures that required more daring risks based on an accurate vision of a changing landscape.

COMPETITION

Competition worked two ways for Amazon.com. At first, the online retailer had to show that it could sell enough books via the Internet to compete with traditional brick-and-mortar stores, particularly the large chains.

Once the company showed that Internet

Hard Work and Luck

In 2001, Jeff Bezos was inducted into the American Academy of Achievement. That year, he discussed his life and Amazon.com in an interview with the academy. One of the questions raised to the entrepreneur was about his ability to see and act on the huge potential of the Internet. Bezos explained that hard work and luck have played a part in Amazon.com's success:

I think there are a couple of things. One of the things everybody should realize is that any time a start-up company turns into a substantial company over the years, there was a lot of luck involved. There are a lot of entrepreneurs. There are a lot of people who are very smart, very hardworking, very few ever have the planetary alignment that leads to a tiny little company growing into something substantial. So that requires not only a lot of planning, a lot of hard work, a big team of people who are all dedicated, but it also requires that not only the planets align, but that you get a few galaxies in there aligning, too. That's certainly what happened to us.[4]

bookselling could be successful, Amazon.com had to be prepared to fight off those same established booksellers, such as Barnes & Noble and Borders, as they began taking Internet sales more seriously. Bezos urged his employees to concentrate on the big picture of keeping their customers happy. He said, "Our secret is that we have not been competitor-obsessed. We have been customer-obsessed."[5] That focus would help the company continue to survive and grow.

By 2001, Amazon.com was up to 35 million customers and $2 billion in sales. Still, Bezos said there were times when the financial situation was so bleak that the company was within 45 days of having to close. During some periods of growth, the more money Amazon.com produced in sales translated into more money in losses to keep up. Costs were higher than Bezos had expected. In part, this was because the responses were more positive than had been imagined. All of these developments simply served as a way of encouraging more risk—sacrificing more of the present—because of the clear signs of what could be there in the future.

During such times, Bezos's ability to convince individual investors of future profits was another

Many Partnerships

The 2001 partnership with Borders Inc. is one of many that Amazon.com has created. Other partners have included Toys "R" Us, the National Basketball Association, the Bombay Company, and Target.

important part of keeping the company viable. But not everyone was convinced. Many who did not buy into the prospects of a bright future for the company often predicted Amazon.com's demise. But their predictions would prove incorrect.

The year 2001 proved to be a positive one for Amazon.com. Not only did the company manage to stay in business, it signed a deal with a competitor. In April 2001, Amazon.com agreed to handle Internet traffic for Borders.

The following January, Amazon.com hit a major milestone. In January 2002, Amazon.com reported its first quarterly profit from the fourth quarter of 2001. Two years later, the company had even better news: 2003 was Amazon.com's first profitable year.

Once a competitor, Borders became Amazon.com's partner in 2001 when Amazon.com took over online retail operations for Borders.

Jeff Bezos stands with one of his door desks.

FOLLOWING THE PLAN

ince launching Amazon.com, Jeff Bezos had made it clear that he wanted to focus on growth rather than profits. However, making money attracts investors, and he needed investments in order to continue focusing on his company and his goals. Amazon.com needed funding to survive until it became a profitable business. The partnership with Kleiner Perkins Caulfield & Byers allowed Bezos to continue to pursue his ideas and build his company.

With sufficient investment to keep his big-picture plan in place, Bezos made sure that his company's focus remained on serving its customers. In November 1997, Amazon.com opened a fulfillment center in New Castle, Delaware. Workers at the vast warehouse would help ensure that Amazon.com customers would receive their orders in a timely manner. The Delaware location would be the first of several centers nationwide.

Bezos also made sure that Amazon.com did not stray from the little things that made the company different. Money was spent liberally when it meant improving processes that would create happy and loyal customers, but it was spent conservatively on comfort items for employees. Most of the desks at Amazon.com were still "door desks."

Filling Orders

As the company grew and orders continued to increase, additional distribution centers were opened in Nevada, Kansas, and Kentucky in 1999.

In 2007, Amazon.com announced plans for a fulfillment center in Indiana. A fulfillment center was opened in Arizona in 2008.

Bezos copied the cheap desks he had put together for himself when the company started, using basic tools to transform a door into a desktop. This was much less expensive than buying desks.

The Work Culture

During Amazon.com's early days of incredible growth, key employees worked very long hours. Many of them had become accustomed to working hours on end to launch the company and make it a success. Bezos and his employees often found themselves faced with the seemingly impossible task of meeting all the orders, but they did not give up. Although they may have felt overwhelmed, Bezos and his staff at Amazon.com were intent on getting orders completed and shipped as quickly as possible. They wanted to keep customers coming back.

Six Core Values

Amazon.com lists six core values for its operation:
- Customer obsession
- Ownership
- Bias for action
- Frugality
- High hiring bar
- Innovation

Bezos developed expectations of his employees being able to handle large volumes of work regularly. Some suggested he believed projects could be done in about half the time they actually took to complete. The company went through heavy turnover of high-ranking people who left to pursue other jobs. His key people, however, remained and established what would become the Amazon.com way of working. When it was time to hire, Bezos believed strongly in the need to get a truly good fit. "I'd rather interview 50 people and not hire anyone than hire the wrong person," Bezos told a colleague during the days of early growth. "Cultures aren't so much planned as they evolve from that early set of people."[1]

When meetings and brainstorming sessions led to talk that the company needed better communication, Bezos insisted that Amazon.com steer away from how that would normally be achieved. He did not want the company bogged down in lengthy discussions on projects without the ability to take action. He talked often about the concept of "two-pizza teams." To be effective, groups had to be small enough that the members could be fed with two large pizzas as they met and talked to work out details. Those groups of five to seven people created many of Amazon.com's key innovations.

The two-pizza teams are an example of how Amazon.com often did not follow a typical organizational chart where the few highest-ranking people make all the big decisions. If a decision was based on facts, Bezos believed it was not necessary for it to come from the top.

APPEALING TO CONSUMERS

Amazon.com grew from its ability to produce new ideas that served customers well. The Web site used cookies in its original programming. These computer files would help recognize customers and steer them toward items they would find interesting when they returned to the Web site.

Consumers were encouraged to contribute to the site. Readers were prompted to submit reviews. Rather than fear

---

Historic Role Models

In a 2001 interview, Jeff Bezos listed Thomas Edison and Walt Disney as the two historical figures he considered as role models. Bezos explained his reasoning:

I've always been interested in inventors and invention. Edison, of course, for a little kid and probably for adults, too, is not only the symbol of that but the actual fact of that—the incredible inventor. I've always felt that there's a certain kind of important pioneering that goes on from an inventor like Thomas Edison. Disney was a different sort of thing. He was also a real pioneer and an inventor, doing new things. It seemed to me that he had this incredible capability to create a vision that he could get a large number of people to share. Things that Disney invented, like Disneyland, the theme parks, they were such big visions that no single individual could ever pull them off, unlike a lot of the things that Edison worked on. Walt Disney really was able to get a big team of people working in a concerted direction.[2]

that negative reviews would hurt the sale of an individual product, the plan was to give customers trusted information to help them feel comfortable making a purchase without searching elsewhere. Visitors to Amazon.com could read other consumers' reviews of books they had purchased. This would help those who had not yet purchased a book decide if it was something they really wanted to invest in. The reviews also helped reviewers feel more of a connection with the Web site.

Word of Mouth

Jeff Bezos has always focused on providing great customer service. He explained, "If you do build a great experience, customers tell each other about that. Word of mouth is very powerful."[3]

In October 2003, Amazon.com launched its Search Inside the Book feature, which allowed visitors to read a portion of approximately 120,000 books online. It was the online equivalent of being in a bookstore and browsing through a title sitting on a shelf. This would help consumers determine whether they really wanted to purchase a book.

Bezos said titles that have the Search Inside the Book feature available have increased sales 9 percent compared to those that do not. He acknowledged concern that books used for reference could have decreased sales—users would not need to buy the

Lucky to Be Alive

Jeff Bezos survived a helicopter crash on March 6, 2003. He and two other passengers were aboard when the pilot ran into trouble with high winds while flying over the rocky, high plains of the area near the Texas ranch where Bezos had spent time as a child. The pilot brought the helicopter in for landing, but the main rotor hit a large tree. The helicopter rolled over and landed in the shallow waters of Calamity Creek. Following cell phone calls from Bezos and another passenger, the U.S. Border Patrol sent a rescue team. Bezos suffered lacerations to his head but he recovered quickly.

book if they could find the needed information with the Search Inside the Book feature. But Bezos said that giving readers a chance to look inside and see what is available has actually boosted sales totals.

Loyal customers were often offered ways to receive better services, all with the hope that they would then use Amazon.com even more. One example was Amazon Prime, a service in which customers could, for a fee of $79 per year, be guaranteed two-day shipping of any product they purchased that year. "We're pleased with our overall strong growth and especially with the number of people joining Amazon Prime," Bezos said.[4]

And this growth would continue. Bezos always thought about possibilities for the site and the consumer. He added features to help the buying process. He would soon make a change that would bring even more users to the site. Knowing others would also try to sell books online, Bezos positioned Amazon.com to sell other products as well.

Jeff Bezos built Amazon.com by focusing on customer service. He wears a sticker showing the company's logo, which has a subtle smile.

Jeff Bezos holds a copy of Fluid Concepts and Creative Analogies *by Douglas Hofstadter. This was the first book sold online by Amazon.com.*

MORE THAN BOOKS

mazon.com's early marketing referred
to the company as "Earth's biggest
bookstore." But books were merely a starting point
for Jeff Bezos when he launched his company.
The computer era helped change how books were

distributed. Bezos saw that the technology used to get Amazon.com started in the book industry could also be useful for other products and other businesses.

Others tried to duplicate what Bezos had done with Amazon.com. Internet businesses began springing up in book and other industries. While this was happening, Bezos was looking in new directions. When it came time to sell more than books, the online bookseller added other media offerings. Music CDs were made available in June 1998. In November, DVDs were added. One year later, toys, electronics, computer software, video games, and home improvement products were added. Clothing lines were sold in partnership with established stores such as the Gap, Nordstrom, and Lands' End. Many of the products someone might find at a grocery or drug store were added later.

International Sites

The year 1998 was one of growth for Amazon.com. In addition to acquiring PlanetAll and Junglee and getting a new space for its headquarters, the company launched two European versions of its site. Amazon.co.uk and Amazon.de began selling books from the United Kingdom and Germany, respectively. Two more international sites launched in 2000: Amazon.fr in France and Amazon.co.jp in Japan. Amazon.ca started selling books in Canada in 2002.

Bezos always seemed to have ideas for his online business, and he was willing to share his ideas and experiences with other businesses. This included his business plan, the massive warehouses he had built to handle Amazon.com's inventory, and more. Amazon.com revealed plans to charge other companies for use of computer storage space and technology used to make their businesses run.

Some investors and analysts wondered about the moves. Rather than use profitable areas of the business to turn money back to investors, Bezos looked at ways to build a stronger future.

A New Space

Online growth required physical expansion for Amazon.com. In August 1998, Bezos leased a former veterans' hospital in Seattle, Washington, to house his company's headquarters.

He dismissed critics, saying that mistakes can just as easily be made by failing to act as they can be by taking another risk. In this case, Amazon.com could look to new ways to make money without making significant new investments. Each step forward, offering new products or making services available to other organizations for a fee, was a chance to further expand the business.

When Amazon.com announced a 38 percent increase in profits

from the first quarter of 2006 to the first quarter of 2007, increased sales in electronics, jewelry, apparel, and shoes were noted as among the reasons for the growth. "This is not about adding new customers," Scott Devitt, an analyst for Stifel, Nicolaus & Company, told the *New York Times*. "It is about increasing purchases from existing customers. The capacity to find what one is looking for on the site has increased significantly, and that is what is driving growth."[1]

SURVIVING TOUGH TIMES

While Amazon.com has grown through the years, there have been some tough times when Bezos ran into doubters and critics. Not all of the doubts were directed at the ideas Bezos had or at Amazon.com itself.

The early boom of dot-com investing led to a crash in the value of businesses that were not generating enough profit on the Internet. By the time the dot-com market crashed, Amazon.com, unlike many of the other start-up companies, was bringing in money. It did, however, still have high expenses. And it carried the stigma of being lumped in with other dot-coms that were not bringing in money and, therefore, were not successful. Even in the early years, when investment money poured in, Amazon.com was still technically operating at a loss, spending significantly more money than it generated. Amazon.com had enough value to survive an extreme drop in its stock prices, but it took some hard hits in the process.

In addition to its financial issues, Amazon.com faced challenges when acquiring smaller companies that developed software that could benefit the Internet retailer. Although the acquisitions often led to programming

Personal Wealth

Jeff Bezos's wealth has fluctuated with the value of Amazon.com's stock. When the company debuted on Wall Street, its stock was valued at $18. On December 10, 1999, the value soared to its peak of $106.69 a share. It later dipped substantially to less than $6 a share in September 2001.

Estimates of Bezos's net worth—the value of his investments and properties minus his debts—soared as high as $10.1 billion in 1999. When the value of dot-com stocks in general crashed in 2000, Amazon.com stock prices plummeted. With much of his personal wealth connected to the Amazon.com stock he still owned, Bezos saw his net worth dip to the lowest it had been since launching his company.

There have been various estimates of Bezos's net worth since. *Forbes* magazine, in its annual rankings of billionaires around the world, placed the entrepreneur's net worth on the rise at $2.5 billion in 2003 and $5.1 billion in 2004. Since then, the figures have dipped and then grown, dropping to $4.3 billion in 2006, and then increasing to $8.2 billion in 2008. In March 2009, *Forbes* noted Bezos's net worth as $6.8 billion.

improvements that boosted overall operation, assessing the value of the changes made through new technology was difficult.

In 1998, Amazon.com purchased PlanetAll and Junglee "to strengthen and broaden the services available at its Web site."[2] Amazon.com purchased three more companies in 2000: Accept.com, Exchange.com, and Alexa.com. The acquisition of Alexa.com led to lawsuits and an investigation by the Federal Trade Commission (FTC). The FTC checked claims that Alexa's programs collected too much information from customers without making it clear enough exactly what was being collected.

Still in Charge

Amazon.com, Google, eBay, and Yahoo! are seen as the companies that changed and developed the Internet. Jeff Bezos is the only founder among that group of companies who continues to run the company as chief executive officer. There have been suggestions at various times that Bezos needs to let trained executives run the company. However, he has always remained a hands-on leader, continuing to be involved in discussions regarding which paths Amazon.com should and will follow next.

Amazon.com also experienced legal battles with its competitors and partners. Competitor Walmart filed a lawsuit claiming that Amazon.com was intentionally hiring away workers with knowledge of Walmart's business practices. The lawsuit was later dropped.

Amazon.com partner Toys "R" Us also filed a lawsuit against the online giant. The companies had agreed that Toys "R" Us would be the exclusive toy and game retailer on Amazon.com. Toys "R" Us accused Amazon.com of breaking that agreement and legally severed its partnership with Amazon.com. This ended the partnership four years before the contract would have ended.

Moon Landing

Jeff Bezos traces his interest in outer space to Neil Armstrong, the U.S. astronaut who became the first person to walk on the moon. That July 20, 1969, event made an impression on the then five-year-old Bezos.

BLUE ORIGIN

As Bezos developed his company into a retailer of a variety of products, he never abandoned the dreams of colonizing space that he had spoken about in his high school graduation valedictory speech. He merely adjusted them.

Amazon.com has made Bezos a wealthy man. One of his major personal investments was in Blue Origin. He started the project in 2000.

Blue Origin is not quite the space colonization plan he spoke about as a teenager, but it does involve

Jeff Bezos bought the Longfellow Ranches in Texas to establish a spaceport for Blue Origin.

space travel in the form of tourism. On January 2, 2007, Bezos wrote about a launch Blue Origin had conducted two months earlier:

> We're working, patiently and step-by-step, to lower the cost of spaceflight so that many people can afford to go and so that we humans can better continue exploring the Solar System. Accomplishing this mission will take a long time, and we're working on it methodically. . . .[3]

Jeff Bezos purchased one of J. K. Rowling's seven handwritten copies of The Tales of Beedle the Bard *in a charity auction.*

HELPING OTHERS

In addition to being able to pursue his interests, the wealth he has achieved through Amazon.com has allowed Bezos to help others through a variety of charitable endeavors. This includes an auction where Bezos purchased a special book. Author J. K. Rowling gave the world the wildly popular Harry Potter series. She also produced a limited edition of seven handwritten and illustrated copies of *The Tales of Beedle the Bard*, a book of children's stories. The book is referred to in *Harry Potter and the Deathly Hallows*, the last book of the Harry Potter series.

Rowling presented six of the books to people close to her for their support in making the Harry Potter series possible. The seventh copy was auctioned off for charity on December 13, 2007. The winning bid came from someone in the book business.

Bezos paid $3.98 million to obtain the final copy of Rowling's *The Tales of Beedle the Bard*. It was the highest auction price ever paid for a modern manuscript. The money was donated to the Children's Voice charity campaign. Bezos talked about Rowling:

> *Even before establishing her charity, J. K. Rowling had done the world a rare and immeasurably valuable service— enlarging forever our concept of the way books can touch people—and in particular children—in modern times.*[4]

Following the auction, the book was published for the general public and released late in 2008. Proceeds from sales of the book went to the Children's High Level Group, the charity that runs the Children's Voice campaign.

Employees Give Back

Amazon.com's charitable work extends beyond Bezos to those who work for him. Amazon.com employees have various community projects that help raise funds where the company has offices. Among the highlights are holiday toy donations in Goodyear, Arizona, the location of a large Amazon.com distribution center. Seattle employees have adopted families in need during the holiday season. They have also held blood and clothing drives. In the Midwest, employees in Coffeyville, Kansas, have organized bake sales to raise money to support the American Cancer Society. And in Huntington, West Virginia, employees have worked together to build houses for Habitat for Humanity.

Bezos has offered his company's Web site and technology to help nonprofit organizations collect donations more easily and has encouraged customers to join in charitable efforts. As a result, customers have contributed millions of dollars to programs providing relief following the 9/11 attacks, the tsunami in Asia in December 2004, and Hurricane Katrina.

Bezos has affected far more than the consumers who visit his site. His ingenuity and determination have helped countless people in need. Those characteristics and Bezos's desire to explore new areas would introduce the world to a method of reading that takes advantage of the technology Bezos loves.

Jeff Bezos reads his favorite children's book, Stinky Cheese Man, to kids in March 2001.

Jeff Bezos uses a projected image of a book to introduce the Kindle at a news conference in 2007.

EXPLORING POSSIBILITIES

*F*or many years after its launch in 1994, Amazon.com sold and distributed other companies' merchandise. Jeff Bezos's creation of Amazon.com made it easier for readers to purchase books. Over the years, Amazon.com expanded by offering a variety of products. In 2007, Bezos revealed that Amazon.com was entering a new area of retail: the company was going to sell its own product.

Amazon.com's next step would be making books more convenient in many ways. Bezos presented the Kindle, a handheld reading device and the latest development in electronic books, called e-books. The Kindle represented Amazon.com's foray into the world of e-books. Such books had been attempted rather unsuccessfully throughout the previous 15 years. In order to make an impact, Amazon.com needed to make the Kindle seem more convenient than books themselves.

Readers can use the Kindle's wireless technology to download and store multiple books. The handheld gadget weighs little more than a half pound (.23 kg), which makes keeping and storing books quite convenient. Users can also adjust font size to their preferences. For example, vision-impaired readers can instantly turn any available book into a large-print version with the use of the Kindle.

The Development of e-Books

The first small-scale attempts at producing e-books date back to the early 1990s. Rocket eBook was released in 1998. Nuvomedia created the Rocket eBook and sold tens of thousands of its devices before ceasing production. In 2000, Stephen King wrote the digital-only novel *Riding Bullet*.

RCA eventually produced later models of the Rocket eBook after Gemstar's buyout of Nuvomedia in 2000.

The invention of e-ink, which made reading on the screen easier and more like reading a book page, helped reopen the e-book market in 2006. One year later, the new Sony Reader used the same e-ink technology seen in Amazon.com's

Building a Library

Amazon.com needed to work with publishers to make sure as many titles as possible were available to read on the Kindle. The process of publishing a modern book often includes a portable document format (PDF) file, which can be transformed into an electronic book rather easily. Older titles, however, are not as readily available. Also, some publishers were slower than others to cooperate as they judged the merits of having electronic versions of their books sold for lower prices than the hardcover versions.

Amazon.com's earlier efforts on its Search Inside the Book feature helped make digital versions of more books available for formatting. Negotiations continued with publishers to free up as many books as possible. The number of available books grew rapidly. More than 180,000 books were available for the Kindle in less than a year. During the process, files were created to make the first chapter of many books available as a free sample.

"The vision for Kindle is every book ever in print in any language—all available in less than 60 seconds," Bezos explained. "Visions take a long time to achieve. It's a bold vision but I think it's a really cool vision and we're excited about it."[1]

Kindle. Sony found enough success to produce an updated version of its e-book reader.

Amazon.com came up with a few new developments. Using wireless technology similar to a cell phone, the Kindle was able to download directly to the unit without the need of a connection to a computer or a wireless Internet hot spot. Customers could download the books and store as many as 200 of them at a time. More could be stored on a memory card, and others were always available for one-minute downloads through the Amazon.com Web site. Amazon.com's account records even keep books available for a new download if, for any reason, they should be erased from a customer's Kindle.

New Avenues

The development of the Kindle was the latest reminder that Amazon.com was determined to continue developing new business ventures under the leadership of Bezos. Rather than settle for the share of the market it held at a given time, the company keeps looking for ways to get bigger. If the Kindle could capture the imagination of dedicated readers, Amazon.com certainly had a captive

Amazon.com's Kindle 2.0

target audience already doing business through the company's Web site.

"If you're going to do something like this, you have to be as good as the book in a lot of respects," Bezos said at the time Amazon.com was preparing to release the first version of the Kindle late in 2007. "But we also have to look for things that ordinary books can't do."[2] Bezos needed to create a clearly readable screen so that reading remained as comfortable on the eyes when using the Kindle as it did when reading a printed page. Long-lasting, rechargeable batteries were necessary to keep from interruptions when reading an e-book. Bezos knew the Kindle could not succeed if it was less convenient than a book, which he considers an extremely effective creation in its original form. "The book just turns out to be an incredible device," Bezos said.[3]

In addition to books, the Kindle can also be used to subscribe to electronic versions of newspapers, magazines, and blogs, which then are updated automatically each time a new issue or entry is published.

Making a Splash

The Kindle's 2007 debut was so successful that it placed the Internet giant in an odd and uncomfortable position. The company was unable to get orders shipped in a timely fashion because it did not have enough Kindles manufactured to meet the original demand. When the units sold out in November, some customers were forced to wait as

The Kindle's Cost

In May 2009, Kindle 2.0 cost $359 each, while Kindle DX cost $489 each. These prices made the technology out-of-reach for some readers. But for those who could afford it, the Kindle could ultimately bring their reading costs down—if they were inclined to make many book purchases in a year. Even the newest books could usually be added to the Kindle for approximately $10 each, with older and less expensive print books costing considerably less to download.

long as six weeks for delivery. All Bezos could do was apologize and hope for their understanding while manufacturing caught up to demand as quickly as possible.

Early in 2008, the home page of Amazon.com included an apology letter from Bezos to the customers.

Dear Customers,

We had high hopes for Kindle before its launch, but we didn't expect the demand that actually materialized. We sold out in the first 5½ hours and have been scrambling [to increase our manufacturing capacity] ever since. We've been shipping on a first-come, first-served basis, but many customers have had to wait as long as six weeks after ordering.

We hope to announce to you within the next few weeks that we're back in stock and that when you order a Kindle, we'll ship it to you that very same day. That's our goal: order today, and we ship today. Until then, customers can order now, and they'll be first in line.

For those of you who've waited six weeks to get your Kindle, you have our sincere thanks for your patience. Many of you have written detailed and thoughtful customer reviews, and we're grateful for that too.[4]

The Kindle needs books to be loaded into it. Before long, customers were ordering those books from Amazon.com to download into their readers. After six months, according to Bezos, more than 6 percent of Amazon.com's book sales were in the form of Kindle downloads. Before a year was up, that number had climbed to more than 10 percent. "We took 14 years building our physical books business," Bezos said. "To have more than 10 percent of unit sales already being Kindle format where we have both [a] Kindle version and a physical version is pretty astonishing to us."[5]

Making Adjustments

Like any electronic device based on a computer program, the first Kindle unit required some adjustments over time. "There will be a first version and a second version and a tenth version," Bezos said.

Promoting Kindle

In 2009, Amazon.com noted the following as part of its description of the Kindle: "At Amazon, we've always been obsessed with having every book ever printed, and we know that even the best reading device would be useless without a massive selection of books. Today, the Kindle Store has more than 270,000 books available, plus top newspapers, magazines, and blogs. This is just the beginning. Our vision is to have every book ever printed, in any language, all available in under 60 seconds on Kindle. We won't stop until we get there."[6]

The popularity of online shopping that Jeff Bezos helped create will likely continue to keep Amazon.com employees busy filling orders.

"It will probably take us 10 years to develop it but you have to get started."[7] A little more than a year after the Kindle debuted, Bezos was on the road promoting the new Kindle 2.0. The latest batch had updated and improved programming. The new version of the Kindle was 8 inches (20.3 cm) long, 5.3 inches (13.5 cm) wide, and .36 inch (.91 cm) thick. The display was 6 inches (15 cm) diagonally. The device weighed 10 ounces (.28 kg) and could store 1,500 books.

In May 2009, the Kindle DX was announced and available for preorder on Amazon.com. The Kindle DX is larger in size and storage capacity than the Kindle 2.0. It is 10.4 inches (26.4 cm) long, 7.2 inches (18.3 cm) wide, and .38 inch (.97 cm) thick. Its screen is 9.7 inches (24.6 cm) diagonally. The Kindle DX weighs 18.9 ounces (.5 kg) and can store 3,500 books.

Those who drive the future of the computer world see more changes ahead. Prior to the Internet era, a company such as Amazon.com was impossible to envision. Bill Hill is the director of advanced reading technologies for Microsoft. He sees a time in the future when the current process of book production, including the resources needed from trees to make paper and fuel to ship products, will seem impractical. "Do you *really* believe that we'll be doing that in 50 years?" Hill said.[8]

Personal Documents

Amazon.com's Kindle does more than allow users to read books, newspapers, and other media. The device also allows users to store, send, and receive personal documents. According to Amazon.com, "Each Kindle has a unique and customizable e-mail address. You can set your unique e-mail address on your Manage Your Kindle page. This allows you and your approved contacts to e-mail Word, PDF documents, and pictures wirelessly to your Kindle for a small per document fee—currently only 10¢ per document."[9]

If not, the significance of the Kindle or similar products will increase and perhaps have a greater impact on the publishing world than what Bezos and Amazon.com have already produced. "This is the most important thing we've ever done," Bezos said. "It's so ambitious to take something as highly evolved as the book and improve on it. And maybe even change the way people read."[10]

Building Inventory

After the company was launched, Amazon.com succeeded through its insistence on offering the best possible service. One of the keys to success in this area was building fulfillment centers to ensure Amazon.com could ship books—and then other products—to customers quickly.

In addition to building its name and success on physical resources, the company has capitalized on technological successes. The databases used to give readers a look inside a book before buying it can

Finding Agreement

Publishers Weekly named Jeff Bezos its Person of the Year for 2008. In an interview with the magazine, Bezos discussed working with publishers, where cooperation helped make Amazon.com's Search Inside the Book and Kindle possible. "I'm extremely pleased and grateful with how supportive publishers have been of our endeavors . . . . Businesses always have complex relationships, and they may not always agree, but at the end of the day, if it's in their mutual interests, they figure out a way to agree."[11]

be useful in making books available for download on the Kindle. While the Kindle is being sold, Amazon.com is building movie databases with the hope of offering customers a quicker way to obtain movies by streaming them instantly over the Internet to customers' computers. When the technology is ready, Amazon.com can be expected to already have a significant number of movies ready to keep a wide variety of customers happy.

WHAT LIES AHEAD

With the Kindle and other projects currently in development, Bezos and Amazon.com may indeed change the way people read and otherwise entertain themselves. His ideas have clearly changed the way people shop. Bezos's creative thinking, hard work, determination, and entrepreneurial spirit have affected countless lives worldwide. His company has led to an enormous array of online buying opportunities for consumers. Amazon.com's Web site has also provided them with opportunities to give to others in need. The company's success has allowed Bezos to do the same.

Bezos has explored retailing books and a wide range of other projects online. Once again, he is

Honorary Doctorate

Jeff Bezos was awarded an honorary doctorate in science and technology from Carnegie Mellon University in 2008.

back to selling books, but this time in a new and innovative format. Bezos has always been a creative thinker who actively pursues possibilities. And although other Internet pioneers have stepped away from running the businesses they have created, Bezos insists he plans to stay involved and continue developing Amazon.com.

While Jeff Bezos may keep adjusting the vision of what lies ahead of him, one can only imagine what the future has in store for the entrepreneurial adventurer. As with his many other endeavors, whatever Bezos pursues will likely be a success for the Internet and publishing pioneer.

The great success of Amazon.com gives Jeff Bezos much to smile about.

TIMELINE

1964	1982	1986
Jeffrey Preston Bezos is born January 12 in Albuquerque, New Mexico.	Bezos graduates from Palmetto High School.	Bezos graduates from Princeton University in the spring.

1995	1996	1997
On July 16, Amazon.com is launched to the public.	A May 16 *Wall Street Journal* story about Amazon.com garners the company new attention.	Amazon.com goes public on May 15, raising $54 million through its initial public offering.

1993	1994	1995
Bezos marries MacKenzie Tuttle.	Bezos moves to Seattle, Washington, to start Amazon.com.	Bezos registers the company name Amazon.com on February 9.

1997	1998	1998
In October, Amazon.com fills its one millionth order. Bezos personally delivers the two books to Japan.	Music CDs and movie DVDs are added to Amazon.com's product list.	In August, Amazon.com leases a former veterans' hospital in Seattle to create its new headquarters.

TIMELINE

1999	1999	1999
Toys, electronics, computer software, video games, and home improvement products are made available on Amazon.com.	*Time* magazine names Bezos its Person of the Year.	Amazon.com stock peaks at $106.69 a share on December 10.

2003	2007	2007
Amazon.com has its first profitable year.	In November, Amazon.com opens its first fulfillment center.	Amazon.com announces plans for the Kindle, its e-book reader.

2001	2002	2003
Amazon.com takes over online sales for Borders.	In January, Amazon.com reports its first quarterly profit from the fourth quarter of 2001.	Search Inside the Book is added to Amazon.com in October.

2007	2007	2009
In November, Amazon.com runs out of Kindles and has to apologize to customers who are forced to wait.	Bezos successfully bids $3.98 million on December 13 to purchase a hand-illustrated book by J. K. Rowling.	In May, Amazon.com announces that the Kindle DX is available for preorder.

Essential Facts

Date of Birth

January 12, 1964

Place of Birth

Albuquerque, New Mexico

Parents

Jackie Gise Bezos and Mike Bezos (adoptive father)

Education

River Oaks Elementary, Palmetto Senior High, Princeton University

Marriage

MacKenzie Tuttle (1993)

Children

Three sons, one daughter

Career Highlights

After graduating from Princeton University in 1986, Bezos worked for Fitel, applying his background in technology and computer science to trading and finance. Within two years, he moved on to Bankers Trust Company, where he became the youngest vice president in company history in 1988. In 1990, Bezos joined D. E. Shaw & Company, where he applied his skills and knowledge to finance and the stock market. In 1994, Bezos left his position to start an online bookstore. Amazon.com was launched in 1995. A love of innovation and determination to provide the best possible service helped the company grow and succeed. Products in dozens of other categories were later added, and the site was also used to raise money for people and organizations in need. The company changed online retailing. In 2007, Amazon.com introduced the Kindle, a wireless device that allows users to download, store, and read books at any location.

Societal Contribution

Amazon.com has changed the way people shop and is changing the way people read. The company has helped online retailing improve and grow. In addition to working on business ventures, Bezos and his employees have given back to communities nationwide through a variety of charitable activities. The Web site has also helped raise millions of dollars for organizations that help those in need.

Conflicts

Amazon.com has had many critics since its launch. Many of them were certain the company would fail. The organization has also faced lawsuits from competitors and partners. Walmart claimed Amazon.com was hiring away employees, while Toys "R" Us sued to end its partnership with Amazon.com early. In 2007, customers who ordered the new Kindle were likely disappointed and frustrated when Amazon.com ran out of the product, which forced customers to wait as long as six weeks for delivery.

Quote

"I've always been at the intersection of computers and whatever they can revolutionize."—*Jeff Bezos*

Additional Resources

Select Bibliography

Deutschman, Alan. "Inside the Mind of Jeff Bezos." *FastCompany. com*. 19 Dec. 2007. 22 Apr. 2009 <http://www.fastcompany.com/ magazine/85/bezos_1.html>.

Frey, Christine, and John Cook. "How Amazon.com survived, thrived and turned a profit." *Seattlepi.com*. 28 Jan. 2004. 22 Apr. 2009 <http://www.seattlepi.com/business/ 158315_amazon28.html>.

Hof, Robert D. "The Torrent of Energy behind Amazon." *BusinessWeek.com*. 14 Dec. 1998. 22 Apr. 2009 <http://www.businessweek.com/1998/50/b3608008.htm>.

Levy, Stephen. "The Future of Reading." *Newsweek.com*. 26 Nov. 2007. 22 Apr. 2009 <http://www.newsweek.com/id/70983>.

Quittner, Joshua. "An Eye On The Future." *Time.com*. 27 Dec. 1999. 22 Apr. 2009 <http://www.time.com/time/magazine/ article/0,9171,992928-9,00.html>.

Further Reading

Landrum, Gene N. *Entrepreneurial Genius: The Power of Passion*. Burlington, ON: Brendan Kelly, 2003.

Leibovich, Mark. *The New Imperialists: How Five Restless Kids Grew Up to Virtually Rule Your World*. New York: Prentice Hall, 2002.

Spector, Robert. *Amazon.com: Get Big Fast*. New York: HarperBusiness, 2000.

Web Links

To learn more about Jeff Bezos, visit ABDO Publishing Company online at **www.abdopublishing.com**. Web sites about Jeff Bezos are featured on our Book Links page. These links are routinely monitored and updated to provide the most current information available.

Places to Visit

Center for the History of Print Culture in Modern America
University of Wisconsin—Madison
600 North Park Street, Madison, WI 53706
608-263-2900
slisweb.lis.wisc.edu/~printcul
The center studies how the printed word has influenced U.S. society.

Computer History Museum
1401 North Shoreline Boulevard, Mountain View, CA 94043
650-810-1010
www.computerhistory.org
The Computer History Museum holds a variety of artifacts relating to the history of computer technology. The museum's exhibits show everything from vintage computers to the earliest calculators.

The Tech Museum of Innovation
201 South Market Street, San Jose, CA 95113
408–294–TECH (8324)
www.thetech.org/info
The museum allows visitors to explore and experience cutting-edge technologies.

Glossary

astronaut
> A person who trains for or takes part in spaceflight.

browser
> A computer program that helps a user locate Web sites on the Internet.

cookie
> A small file stored on a computer after a user visits a Web site. It provides information, such as a record of pages visited, to the Web site during later visits.

dot-com
> An Internet company.

e-book
> An electronic book.

entrepreneur
> A person who starts a business.

e-tailer
> One who sells goods electronically using the Internet.

first-phase automation
> The process of making technology work faster and more efficiently.

insolvent
> Having debts greater than the value of items owned.

Internet
> A network through which computers around the world are connected.

Ivy League
> A group of prestigious colleges and universities in the northeastern United States, consisting of Brown, Columbia, Cornell, Dartmouth, Harvard, the University of Pennsylvania, Princeton, and Yale.

Nobel Prize
> One of many annual prizes awarded for outstanding achievement in physics, chemistry, medicine or physiology, literature, and the promotion of peace.

physics
> A science that deals with matter, energy, motion, and force.

refugee
> A person who flees a country for safety, often during times of war or political upheaval.

second-phase automation
> The process of changing the underlying way business processes are performed.

stock market
> A market where stocks and bonds are traded or exchanged.

tsunami
> An unusually large sea wave produced by a seaquake or undersea volcanic eruption.

valedictorian
> The student who ranks highest academically in a graduating class.

venture capitalist
> A person who gives money to people to help them pursue innovative projects.

Wall Street
> A street in New York City that serves as the financial center of the U.S. stock market.

SOURCE NOTES

Chapter 1. Mapping Out a Plan
1. Alan Deutschman. "Inside the Mind of Jeff Bezos." *FastCompany.com*. 19 Dec. 2007. 22 Apr. 2009 <http://www.fastcompany.com/magazine/85/bezos_4.html>.
2. Joshua Quittner. "An Eye on the Future." *Time.com*. 27 Dec. 1999. 21 Apr. 2009 <http://www.time.com/time/printout/0,8816,992928,00.html>.
3. "Jeff Bezos Interview." *Achievement.org*. American Academy of Achievement. 4 May 2001. 22 Apr. 2009 <http://www.achievement.org/autodoc/printmember/bez0int-1>.
4. Ibid.
5. Ibid.

Chapter 2. Young Jeff
1. Gene N. Landrum. *Entrepreneurial Genius: The Power of Passion*. Burlington, ON: Brendan Kelly, 2004. 277–278.
2. Chip Bayers. "The Inner Bezos." *Wired.com*. 2004. 11 May 2009 <http://www.wired.com/wired/archive/7.03/bezos_pr.html>.
3. Gene N. Landrum. Entrepreneurial Genius: The Power of Passion. Burlington, ON: Brendan Kelly, 2004. 278.

Chapter 3. Education
1. Robert D. Hof. "The Torrent of Energy Behind Amazon." *Businessweek.com*. 14 Dec. 1998. 22 Apr. 2009 <http://www.businessweek.com/1998/50/b3608008.htm>.
2. Gene N. Landrum. *Entrepreneurial Genius: The Power of Passion*. Burlington, ON: Brendan Kelly, 2004. 279.
3. Chip Bayers. "The Inner Bezos." *Wired.com*. 2004. 22 Apr. 2009 <http://www.wired.com/wired/archive/7.03/bezos_pr.html>.
4. Phi Beta Kappa Society. "The Nation's Oldest and Most Widely Known Academic Honor Society." *PBK.org*. 21 Apr. 2009 <http://www.pbk.org/infoview/PBK_InfoView.aspx?t=&id=8>.

Chapter 4. Finding Work and Love

1. Gene N. Landrum. *Entrepreneurial Genius: The Power of Passion*. Burlington, ON: Brendan Kelly, 2004. 281.

2. Joshua Quittner. "An Eye on the Future." *Time.com*. 27 Dec. 1999. 21 Apr. 2009 <http://www.time.com/time/printout/0,8816,992928,00. html>.

3. Brian Miller. "Profile: MacKenzie Bezos." *SeattleWeekly.com*. 14 Sept. 2005. 22 Apr. 2009 <http://www.seattleweekly.com/2005-09-14/arts/ profile-mackenzie-bezos.php>.

4. "About the Book: Testing of Luther Albright, The." *HarperCollins. com*. 5 Sept. 2006. 22 Apr. 2009 <http://www.harpercollins.com/ books/9780061249570/The_Testing_of_Luther_Albright/index.aspx>.

5. John Marshall. "Bezos discusses her debut novel and her love for her husband's laugh." *Seattlepi.com*. 26 Aug. 2005. 22 Apr. 2009 <http://www. seattlepi.com/books/238032_book26.html>.

Chapter 5. Following a Dream

1. "Jeff Bezos Interview." *Academy of Achievement*. 4 May 2001. 22 Apr. 2009 <http://www.achievement.org/autodoc/printmember/bez0int-1>.

2. Gene N. Landrum. *Entrepreneurial Genius: The Power of Passion*. Burlington, ON: Brendan Kelly, 2004. 284.

3. Ibid.

4. "Jeff Bezos Interview." *Academy of Achievement*. 4 May 2001. 22 Apr. 2009 <http://www.achievement.org/autodoc/printmember/bez0int-1>.

5. Ibid.

6. Ibid.

7. Chris Anderson. "The Zen of Jeff Bezos." *Wired.com*. Jan. 2005. 22 Apr. 2009 <http://www.wired.com/wired/archive/13.01/bezos.html>.

8. "Jeff Bezos Interview." *Academy of Achievement*. 4 May 2001. 22 Apr. 2009 <http://www.achievement.org/autodoc/printmember/bez0int-1>.

Chapter 6. Creating a Successful Product

1. Gene N. Landrum. *Entrepreneurial Genius: The Power of Passion*. Burlington, ON: Brendan Kelly, 2004. 273.

2. Ibid.

3. Chris Anderson. "The Zen of Jeff Bezos." *Wired.com*. Jan. 2005. 22 Apr. 2009 <http://www.wired.com/wired/archive/13.01/bezos.html>.

Source Notes Continued

Chapter 7. Business Success

1. Rich Karlgaard. "Digital Rules: Coming Soon—Cyber Co-Ops." *Forbes.com*. 28 Dec. 1998. 22 Apr. 2009 <http://www.forbes.com/forbes/1998/1228/6214043a.html>.
2. Chris Anderson. "The Zen of Jeff Bezos." *Wired.com*. Jan. 2005. 22 Apr. 2009 <http://www.wired.com/wired/archive/13.01/bezos.html>.
3. "Jeff Bezos Biography." *Achievement.org*. American Academy of Achievement. 28 Nov. 2007. 22 Apr. 2009 <http://www.achievement.org/autodoc/printmember/bezobio-1>.
4. "Jeff Bezos Interview." *Achievement.org*. American Academy of Achievement. 4 May 2001. 22 Apr. 2009 <http://www.achievement.org/autodoc/printmember/bez0int-1>.
5. Gene N. Landrum. *Entrepreneurial Genius: The Power of Passion*. Burlington, ON: Brendan Kelly, 2004. 273.

Chapter 8. Following the Plan

1. Alan Deutschman. "Inside the Mind of Jeff Bezos." *FastCompany.com*. 19 Dec. 2007. 22 Apr. 2009 <http://www.fastcompany.com/magazine/85/bezos_4.html>.
2. "Jeff Bezos Interview." *Achievement.org*. American Academy of Achievement. 28 Nov. 2007. 22 Apr. 2009 <http://www.achievement.org/autodoc/printmember/bez0int-1>.
3. "Jeff Bezos on Word-of-Mouth Power." *Businessweek.com*. 2 Aug. 2004. 22 Apr. 2009 <http://www.businessweek.com/magazine/content/04_31/b3894101.htm>.
4. Brad Stone. "Both Sales and Earnings Rise Sharply at Amazon." *New York Times Online*. 25 Apr. 2007. 22 Apr. 2009 <http://www.nytimes.com/2007/04/25/technology/25amazon.html>.

Chapter 9. More than Books

1. Brad Stone. "Both Sales and Earnings Rise Sharply at Amazon." *New York Times Online*. 25 Apr. 2007. 22 Apr. 2009 <http://www.nytimes.com/2007/04/25/technology/25amazon.html>.
2. Sandeep Junnarkar. "Amazon to buy two companies." *CNET.com*. 4 Aug. 1998. 14 May 2009. <http://news.cnet.com/Amazon-to-buy-two-companies/2100-1001_3-214057.html?tag=mncol>.
3. Jeff Bezos. "Development Flight, and We are Hiring."*BlueOrigin.com*. 2 Jan. 2007. 15 May 2009 <http://public.blueorigin.com/letter.htm>.

4. "Amazon buys J.K. Rowling tales for $4 million." *ZDNet.com*. 14 Dec. 2007. 22 Apr. 2009 <http://news.zdnet.com/ 2100-9588_22-180372.html>.

Chapter 10. Exploring Possibilities
1. Staci D. Kramer. "Bezos on Kindle: 'We Would Love to Have Color'— And Every Book Ever," *PaidContent.org*. 2 June 2008. 22 Apr. 2009 <http://www.paidcontent.org/entry/419-bezos-on-kindle-we-would- love-to-have-color-and-every-book-ever/>.
2. Steven Levy. "The Future of Reading." *Newsweek.com*. 26 Nov. 2007. 22 Apr. 2009 <http://www.newsweek.com/id/70983>.
3. Ibid.
4. Joshua Topolsky. "Jeff Bezos posts Kindle apology on Amazon's front page." *Engadget.com*. 20 Mar. 2008. 22 Apr. 2009 <http://www.engadget. com/2008/03/20/jeff-bezos-posts-kindle-apology-on-amazons-front- page/>.
5. David LaGesee. "Jeff Bezos on Amazon Kindle and Digital Media." *U.S. News and World Report Online*. 29 Oct. 2008. 22 Apr. 2009 <http://www.usnews.com/articles/business/technology/2008/10/ 29/jeff-bezos-on-amazon-kindle-and-digital-media.html>.
6. "Kindle 2: Amazon's New Wireless Reading Device (Latest Generation)." *Amazon.com*. 2009. 22 Apr. 2009 <http://www. amazon.com/dp/B00154JDAI/?tag=googhydr-20&hvadid=&ref=pd_ sl_18mqco62ua_e>.
7. Staci D. Kramer. "@ D6: Jeff Bezos: Kindle Contributes 6 Percent Of Title Sales." *PaidContent.org*. 2 June 2008. 22 Apr. 2009 <http://www. paidcontent.org/entry/419-d6-jeff-bezos>.
8. Steven Levy. "The Future of Reading." *Newsweek*. 26 Nov. 2007. 22 Apr. 2009 <http://www.newsweek.com/id/70983>.
9. "Kindle 2: Amazon's New Wireless Reading Device (Latest Generation)." *Amazon.com*. 2009. 22 Apr. 2009 <http://www. amazon.com/dp/B00154JDAI/?tag=googhydr-20&hvadid=&ref=pd_ sl_18mqco62ua_e>.
10. Steven Levy. "The Future of Reading." *Newsweek*. 26 Nov. 2007. 22 Apr. 2009 <http://www.newsweek.com/id/70983>.
11. Jim Milliot. "PW's Person of the Year: Jeff Bezos." *Publishers Weekly Web site*. 8 Dec. 2008. 26 May 2009 <http://www.publishersweekly.com/ article/CA6620239.html>.

INDEX